Locally known as Patwa, the Kwéyòl language comes from an influence of mainly French but also English, Spanish and African native languages. Having many similarties to other varieties of Creole, spoken in countries such as, Haiti, Martinique and Guadeloupe, this strand of Creole is mainly spoken in the sister islands of Saint Lucia and Dominica.

This series of books seeks to preserve the deep cultural essence of the Kwéyòl language and it's influence for furture generations. Within this book you will find the Kwéyòl term for familiar animals and the English translation. Each page includes an image to develop you and your family's use of Kwéyòl.

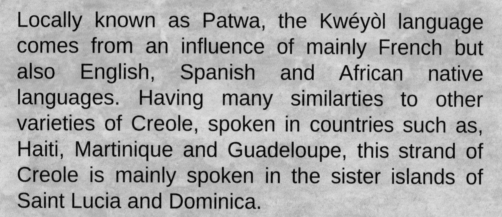

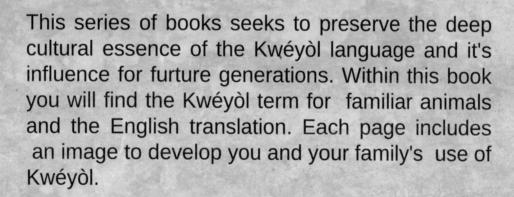

Alligator

Kayman

Ant

Fonmi

Bat

Sòlsouwi

Bee

Myèl or *Vonvon*

Bird

Jibyé

Butterfly

Papiyòt

Camel

Kanmèl

Cat

Chat

Caterpillar

Chini

Chicken

Poul

Cockroach

Wavèt

Cow

Bèf

Dog

Chyen

Dolphin

Dowad

Donkey

Bouwik

Dragonfly

Mawisosé

Eagle

Lèg

Eel

Zandji
Konng (salt-water & moray eel)

Elephant

Léfan

Firefly

Bètafé

Fish

Pwéson

Flea

Pis

Fly

Mouch

Giraffe

Jiraf

Goat

Kabwit

Horse

Cheval

Leech

Sansi

Lion

Lyon

Lizard

Zanndoli

Monkey

Makak

Mouse

Souwi

Octopus

Poulp

Opossum

Mannikou

Owl

Chwèt

Parrot

Jako

Pig

Cochon

Rabbit

Lapen

Rat

Wat

Scorpion

Èskoupyon

Sheep

Mouton

Slug

Bèt san zo or

Vyann san zo

Snail

Kalmason

Snake

sèpan

Squid

Chès

Termite

Poulbwa

Tiger

Tig

Whale

Balenn

Worm

Vè

Other books in this series:

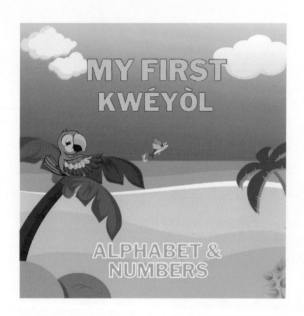

Black Gold Publishing

More books coming soon

Printed in Great Britain
by Amazon

75651021R00029